DONCASTER ROVERS

A PICTORIAL HISTORY

TONY BLUFF & STEVE UTTLEY

AMBERLEY

ACKNOWLEDGEMENTS

Special thanks to Barry Watson, Paul Gilligan, Phil Ryan, John Ryan, Howard Roe, Kate Evans, Maz Ahmed, and all the photographers who have covered Rovers from the early days at the Intake Ground.

First published 2013

Amberley Publishing
The Hill, Stroud
Gloucestershire, GL5 4EP

www.amberleybooks.com

British Library Cataloguing in Publication Data.
A catalogue record for this book is available from the British Library.

ISBN 978 1 4456 1448 9 (print)
ISBN 978 1 4456 1463 2 (ebook)

Typeset in 10pt on 12pt Sabon.
Typesetting and Origination by Amberley Publishing.
Printed in the UK.

DONCASTER ROVERS
A PICTORIAL HISTORY

Doncaster Rovers Football Club was formed one day in September 1879, when an eighteen-year-old fitter at the plant works, Mr Albert Jenkins, was asked by a teacher at the Yorkshire Deaf & Dumb Institution to get a team of young men together to play a football match against boys from the institution. This he did, and by half-time the deaf school were four goals up. Some well-chosen words and positional changes for the second half brought four goals for the Jenkins XI and time was called on a drawn game.

Exhilarated by the exercise and endeavour, along with the camaraderie of playing a football match, they set off on the walk back to town. As they reached the Hall Cross on Bennetthorpe they took a rest and decided to form a football team to play regular games, eventually settling on the name of Doncaster Rovers.

A committee was formed to run the club and select the team; Albert Jenkins took on the role as secretary, as well as acting as captain of the team. It was purely an amateur concern, as it was with all clubs at that time. To raise money, players, and later members of the club, paid a yearly subscription. While their contemporaries were apparently satisfied to play and stay at a local level, the Rovers were obviously ambitious, because they were not satisfied just to play on open fields, which they had to do in the first few years. They wanted a ground of their own that they could enclose and for which they could charge an entrance fee.

In 1885, they obtained the use of a field behind the Yorkshire Institute for the Deaf & Dumb where they could build into their own ground. Known in the first season as the Deaf & Dumb Ground, it became known in succeeding seasons as the Intake Ground, named after the farm that stood where the old fire station stood on Leger Way.

On 25 July 1885, the FA legalised professionalism, subject to certain restrictions. At this point it did not concern the Rovers, but in October 1887 they obtained the services of Sam Hunt, a well-known local footballer who was a professional with Mexborough. He became the first professional to play for the Rovers.

In 1888/89, they finally entered the FA Cup. This had been started in 1871 by the London-based Football Association, which everyone accepted as the ruling body of football. They were drawn to play Rotherham Town in the first qualifying round, at the Intake Ground. Unfortunately, the Rotherham team was far superior and ran out winners by nine goals to one, with Sam Hunt scoring the Rovers' goal. This showed how far the Rovers had to go to catch up with the more established teams.

The earliest known team picture of Doncaster Rovers from 1884/85.

Other than the FA Cup and local cup competitions, all the games played by all clubs were friendlies. Then, in April 1888, football took a giant step forward with the formation of the Football League, the first such organisation in the world. In 1889/90 the Midland Counties League was formed, but the Rovers were not yet ready for that competition. However, they, along with nine other clubs, formed the Midland Alliance in June 1890 at a meeting in Nottingham. The other clubs were: Rotherham Swifts, Notts Olympic, Notts Jardines, Newark, Loughborough Town, Heanor Town, Notts County Rovers, Grantham Rovers and Sheffield FC. However, during the season, Rotherham Swifts and Notts Jardines withdrew. The Rovers finished in second place behind Notts County Rovers. On Saturday 21 March 1891, the club won their first trophy when they beat the two-year-old Sheffield United at Bramall Lane in the final of the Sheffield & Hallamshire FA Cup.

In June 1891 the Rovers joined the Midland Counties League, and after struggles on the field and financially off it, in 1896/97 they built a team good enough to win the competition, following a fierce battle with Glossop North End. They were champions again in 1898/99, and this gave them the confidence to seek election to Division Two of the Football League in May 1900 – but their application for membership was rejected when they received only five votes.

The first ever trophy won by Doncaster Rovers, the Sheffield Challenge Cup, 1890/91. From left to right, back row: Cuthbert, Mr J. Le Brun (committee), Massey, McDonald (trainer), Grey, Mr W. Reid (committee), Parr, James, Mr J. Musson (secretary), Pilkington. Front row: Kisby, McCullum, Langton, Herod, Gresham.

Doncaster Rovers, champions of the Midland League for the second time, 1898/99. From left to right, back row: Eggett (goal), Mr Barrass (vice president), Mr J. Hewitt, Turner (full-back), Langton (full-back), Mr Rogerson (committee), Linward (outside-left), W. Attree (trainer). Middle row: Nelson (outside-right), Longden (right-half), Hulley (centre-half), E. Wright (left-half). Front row: Oxspring (inside-right), Clayton (centre), Gall (inside-left).

They tried again in 1901 to get into the Football League, and after initially failing they were invited in early September, as the club with the most votes among those rejected at the League's AGM, to join the Football League and take the place and fixtures of New Brighton Tower, who had folded and resigned from the Football League Division Two. They accepted the move up the ladder and did well to finish seventh in the eighteen-strong division. Alas, the following season, 1902/03, they finished third from the bottom and had to apply for re-election, which was not forthcoming. The two clubs below them, Stockport County and Burnley, were re-elected, and Bradford City replaced the Rovers.

It was back to the Midland League in 1903/04 for the Rovers and eleventh place in the table at the end of the season. Even with this indifferent season behind them, they applied for admission to the Football League and succeeded (one suspects because of a sympathy vote) in ousting Stockport County for season 1904/05. Having succeeded in regaining their Football League status, their next move was incorporation as a limited company. There was no opposition to this, so Doncaster Rovers Football & Athletic Club Ltd was incorporated on 1 July 1904, with a capital of £1,000, which was divided into 2,000 ordinary shares of 10s (50p) each. The first directors were Mr S. Balmforth, Councillor M. Dowson, Mr H. Athron, Mr F. Richardson, Mr R. S. Dawson and Mr W. E. Rogerson, all prominent businessmen in the town. Mr John Fowler was appointed secretary.

The quality of the team in practice for the 1904/05 season had looked good, but in the League games it was found wanting; the quality of football from the Rovers was abysmal even by Midland League standards. This was never overcome throughout the season, despite the signing of new players. The season progressed on the back of a string of defeats and finished with a record total of just eight points from thirty-four games, in which twenty-three goals were scored and eighty-one conceded, which spoke volumes. The club finished the season in debt to the tune of £260, a large sum in those days. Despite this, the club decided to apply for re-election to Division Two but were firmly pushed out into the cold with only four votes.

Back in the Midland League in 1905, the club struggled on the field and financially over the succeeding seasons. The only highlight came in 1911/12, when the club finished third behind Rotherham County and Rotherham Town in the Midland League, and won the Sheffield & Hallamshire FA Challenge Cup, which they had last won in 1891. They met Sheffield United Reserves in the final at Wath-upon-Dearne, and scored three goals without reply. The financial situation, however, got worse over the next few seasons and became critical in May 1914. Although certain gentlemen of the town had been found to put money down to keep football going, they were unwilling to take over the debts of the old club. On advice from the highest authority, the club was voluntarily wound up on 27 August 1914 and a new club under the same name was formed to carry on in the Midland League. On 3 November 1914, a new company – Doncaster Rovers Limited – was registered to take over the assets and liabilities of the Doncaster Rovers Football & Athletic Club. The nominal capital was £500 in 10s shares. Their final league position in 1914/15 was fifteenth, and a loss of £290 was reported on the season, due in no small measure to the outbreak of war.

Above: A photograph of a Rovers side in 1904. It is not known if this is a first-team shot. It was probably taken in front of the stand at the Intake Ground.

Right: Thomas Bennett of Doncaster Rovers in 1903/04.

Thomas Holmes, goalkeeper for Doncaster Rovers, 1903/04.

Tommy Tompkins of Doncaster Rovers, 1903/04.

Ellis Wright of Doncaster Rovers, 1903/04.

Jimmy Dyer of Doncaster Rovers, 1903/04.

John Murphy of Doncaster Rovers, 1903/04.

Andy Gordon of Doncaster Rovers, 1903/04.

Right: Charles Laverick of Doncaster Rovers, 1903/04.

Below: Poster for Harry Roberts's Benefit, April 1909.

The Midland League was closed down on 31 July 1915 until the war was over. But a group of clubs – Doncaster Rovers, Goole Town, Halifax Town, Rotherham County, Sheffield United Reserves, Worksop Town, Silverwood Colliery and Chesterfield Town – formed the Midland Combination.

By November 1915, the Rovers were unable to raise a team from their own players, who had, in the main, joined the forces, and so they drafted in members of the Durham Light Infantry, who were stationed in the town. However, on 22 July 1916, at a meeting of the clubs in Sheffield, the Midland Combination was abandoned because of a lack of clubs willing to compete, and Doncaster Rovers closed down for the duration of the war.

The club was not resurrected until April 1920, when a number of football enthusiasts called a meeting of like-minded souls in the Cleveland Café. However, they were later advised that because of legal difficulties an entirely new company should be formed. It was decided that the capital should be £10,000, which was to be raised by 10s shares. The Rovers were accepted for the FA Cup and for membership of the Sheffield & Hallamshire FA. A ground seemed to be the only problem, as the Intake was still occupied by the military.

The Corporation had been approached for assistance in finding a suitable site for a ground. On Tuesday 1 June 1920, a club deputation met the Corporation Estates Committee. After putting their views across, they were taken to a field on the Low Pastures of about 6 acres' extent, which the committee was prepared to offer the club at a nominal rent. As it would take some time to get the ground ready, the Corporation agreed to allow the club to use the Education Committee's playing fields at Belle Vue, Bennetthorpe, where Nuttall's Cottages stand today, for the forthcoming season. The club would share the use and the cost with the Education Committee.

At the AGM of the Midland League on 12 June 1920, the Rovers topped the poll for the election of four clubs from the eleven that applied. The stage was now set for the new company to be floated. On 24 June the old company was wound up and the following day a new company was formed, being registered on 13 September as Doncaster Rovers Football Club (1920) Ltd (170192), with a capital of £10,000 in 10s shares. The directors were Messrs Arthur Thomson (contractor) as chairman, Joseph Franks JP, H. G. Fogg, W. A. Curtis and R. W. Merriman. The secretary was Mr Fletcher Hibbert of Messrs Newsum & Co. Meanwhile, an old Rovers player, Billy Calder, offered to act as honorary manager and form a team from the numerous applications that flooded in from prospective players.

On Saturday 26 August 1922, Mr Charles E. Sutcliffe of the Football League performed the formal opening of their new ground on the Low Pastures, unlocking the gates with a silver presentation key. The opposition for the first match on the ground following the opening ceremony was Gainsborough Trinity, in the initial Midland League match of the season. In front of around 10,000, the biggest crowd ever to see a football match in Doncaster, the first goal on the new ground took only seven minutes to arrive when Charlesworth headed in a fine cross by Rintoul. This proved to be the only goal of the match, but it set the Rovers off on the right foot. They gained sixty-one points, a total that had won the championship comfortably in the previous season, but was now two points behind Sheffield Wednesday Reserves. This position was enough for the clubs in the Third Division to vote the Rovers into Division Three North.

Doncaster Rovers, Sheffield Challenge Cup winners for the second time, 1911/12. From left to right, back row: H. Pearce (trainer), Lowe, Shreeve, H. Bromage, Gregory, Nuttall, Taylor. Front row: Woodruffe, Dyal, Reed, Astill, W. Bromage.

Doncaster Rovers 1914/15 in the Midland League; names not known.

Public practice pre-season match between the Reds (on the right) and Blues on Doncaster Rovers' new ground, Belle Vue, August 1922.

Doncaster Rovers first-team players and club officials, pictured before the first match on Belle Vue, 26 August 1922. From left to right, standing: H. G. Fogg (director), A. E. Porter (secretary), W. Dowson (director), J. Franks (chairman), W. Russell (trainer), McLean, McLeod, Mr R. Capes (director), Smithurst, Mr R. W. Merriman (director), Miller, Mr R. H. Hepworth (director), Wigglesworth, Jackson, and A. Thompson, J. C. Morris and F. J. Tighe (directors). Sitting: Rintoul, Jacklin, Ashmore, Boardman, Charlesworth.

A new era was opening up for Doncaster Rovers. The Rovers were back where they felt they belonged, in the Football League. At the club's AGM, a loss of £307 had been reported on the previous season's working, a shortfall due mainly to the expense in moving grounds and to the increased wages and bonuses inherent in providing a team that had done so well. Another unforeseen point also arose due to their league elevation; they had been drawn to play in the early rounds of the FA Cup, but as this would disrupt the fixtures, they withdrew from the competition altogether.

On Saturday 25 August 1923, the Rovers played their first match back in the Football League, at home to Wigan Borough. Before a record crowd of 10,923, who paid £598 in receipts, a fairly even match ended in a goalless draw. The final placing of ninth was very satisfactory in their first season against new opposition. A loss of £46 was reported, with some disquiet expressed at an average gate of 6,500, a figure below what was required to break even. The club's creditors were now owed a total of £1,487.

Financial problems became the norm throughout the 1920s and '30s, with industrial problems in the 1920s and the Depression in the 1930s, so that the only way to keep a balance was to repeatedly sell their best players – and it was an impressive list.

Several times between the First and Second World Wars the record attendance was broken, but they were the highs set against many lows. In 1931/32 the gate receipts were the lowest on record for the club, causing a deficit on the balance sheet at the end of the season of £238 – and it was only that figure because of the transfers of Jim Smith, Joe Bowman, Les Lievesley and John Moody.

In 1934/35, the management were so convinced that they had a successful team that they retained eighteen players and paid them summer wages, not something done in previous seasons. In April 1935, Doncaster Rovers played Tranmere Rovers, another team going for promotion, at home on a Thursday afternoon, before a record crowd of 23,238. The following weekend was Easter. On Good Friday, they were at home to middle-of-the-table Rotherham United in a sensational match played before a new record crowd of 27,554 that ended in Rotherham winning by 5-3. While this win dented the Rovers' hopes, they were still in the driving seat with games in hand. On Easter Saturday they travelled to Tranmere to play a side fading out of the promotion picture and gained a much desired win. A record crowd of 20,357 was at Rotherham to see the Rovers complete their Easter programme on the Monday, and they did it in style with a 3-1 win and a lead at the top of the table, which they held to the end to gain promotion to the Second Division. A profit was reported of £1,753 on the season, with the balance sheet showing the club to be clear of debt and with a sum in hand of £656. Attendances has nearly doubled, with the average attendance rising to 10,681, and as a result no players had been transferred.

In their first season back in the Second Division they were in second place in the table by Christmas on goal average, behind Leicester City. However, the second half of the season produced only two wins and nine points, but at least they were still in Division Two. They also had a new attendance record when on Good Friday they entertained Sheffield United before a crowd of 28,560, who witnessed a goalless draw. The club reported a profit of £2,579, and for the first time in a number of years, shareholders received a dividend of 5 per cent. An average attendance of 14,077 had helped the club to pay transfer fees for players without having to sell anyone to survive.

The club's first venture into a wider sphere came in early December, when they entertained one of Europe's best teams, FC Austria of Vienna. The Austrians surprised everyone with their skill and accuracy of passing, with the Rovers having to get used to 'not charging', especially on the goalkeeper, a policy not employed in the English game for some years to come. The Austrians went ahead after five minutes, but Albert Turner equalised from a penalty. Turner had another chance to score from a penalty in the second half, but he hit the post, the ball going behind. Only three minutes were left when the Austrians scored a winner. A crowd of 3,700 on a Monday afternoon would hardly have paid the guarantee for the visitors, but it was certainly an experience for players and fans alike.

So, there was a certain amount of optimism when the 1936/37 season kicked off under a new manager, Fred Emery. However, despite the signing of a number of players throughout the season, the results did not improve. They remained at the bottom of the table and were eventually relegated together with Bradford City.

On 21 October 1936, the Rovers made club history by accepting an invitation to play the Dutch National XI at the Sparta Rotterdam Stadium – the first time the club had played abroad. The Dutch were preparing for a match against Austria and won 7-2, with centre-forward Bakhuys scoring five goals. The Rovers were not too impressed by the referee, claiming that two of Backhuys' goals were offside and that a disallowed goal by Albert Turner was a legitimate one. One Dutch newspaper was not impressed with the Rovers' display, calling it 'holiday football' and the players 'a bunch of comedians from the English Second and Third Division'. The Rovers also had their first taste of substitute players when Kilhourhy replaced the injured McMahon at half-time. A month later, the Rovers entertained Gradjanski FC from Zagreb, Yugoslavia, who were bolstered by several international players from other clubs in Yugoslavia. The Rovers, with several reserves, won an exciting exhibition match 6-4, after leading 2-0 at half-time.

Although the season was a disaster from the playing point of view, the club still returned a profit of £119 on the season. For once the club paid out more in transfer fees, £6,285, than the £5,500 they had received. But by careful financial management, even a drop in the average gate to 11,697 had not had too detrimental an effect.

It was back to the Third North for the Rovers in 1937/38, finishing in second place, two points adrift of the champions, Tranmere Rovers. In those days only the champions were promoted. An average attendance of 13,040 showed that a successful team could be accommodated in the town. A profit of £465 was the end result of the season's workings, and optimism was high that the club could go one better in 1938/39. However, second place was again achieved, with the club finishing eleven points behind the champions, Barnsley. The fifty-six points that the Rovers had gained would have been enough in previous seasons to ensure promotion, but this particular one had seen Barnsley in splendid form, equalling the Third North record for points gained. After a successful season on the playing side, it was a bit disappointing to report that attendances were down overall to an average of 11,629, although it didn't help having a runaway winner of the division. However, a profit of £546 was reported due to transfer dealings. A dividend of 5 per cent was paid to shareholders for the fourth time.

Above: What did the papers say? The players read the papers.

Right: Four Rovers players dressed to kill in 1925/26. From left to right, standing: Joe Bowman and Jack Buckley. Seated: Charles Smith and Harold Keetley.

Left: Tommy Keetley, 1920: record league goalscorer for Doncaster Rovers with 180 goals.

Below: Doncaster Rovers, 1927/28.

Doncaster Rovers, 1928/29.

Doncaster Rovers, 1930/31.

Belle Vue, 1930/31.

Doncaster Rovers, 1932/33. Left to right, back row: Wilkinson (assistant trainer), Hunter, France, Tate, Walker, Wilkins, Schofield, McLean (trainer). Middle row (players only): Shaw, W. Smith, Flowers, Gladwin, Foster, McHale, Martin, Yeardley, Emery. Front Row: Beynon, Kelly, Renshaw, Atherton, Potter, Waterston, Beresford, R. Smith, Parker, Hargreaves.

Britain declared war on Germany on 3 September 1939, and the Football League suspended their competition after just three games. All players' contracts were suspended, with the result that all of the Rovers players dispersed to the various work of national importance to which they had been assigned. Ten days after the suspension of all football, the Rovers directorate met and decided they would carry on as a football club. Then the FA, after consultation with the Home Office, decided to support the organisation of both friendly and competitive matches on Saturdays and public holidays, provided they were based on a local and district group of clubs and did not interfere with national war work. The Rovers continued to play friendly games until the Football League organised regional leagues for the clubs. As the war progressed, the Football League reorganised their programme on a bigger regional basis, with a cup competition on a small group basis in the qualifying round, the winners going into the competition proper. The Rovers used guest players throughout the war, as did all the other clubs.

The Rovers' best season was in 1944/45 in the War Cup qualifying competition. They won seven of their ten games to qualify for the competition proper. In the competition proper each round was played on a two-leg basis. Getting by Bradford PA in the first round, their next opponents were the cup favourites, Derby County, a very strong combination. The first leg, at home before 23,899 excited spectators, was an even game, with the only difference being Raich Carter, the Sunderland and England inside-left, who was the architect behind the one-goal lead that Derby took home. In the second leg, which Carter missed, the Rovers outplayed Derby to a 4-1 win so that they went through on aggregate to meet Manchester United in the last eight of the competition. The first leg, at home before a big crowd of 29,177, saw United strike twice in the first half-hour and then sit back on their lead. Jordan pulled a goal back four minutes into the second-half but, despite constant pressure, could not pierce United's defence again. The return match, played at Maine Road (Manchester City's ground) because Old Trafford had suffered bomb damage, was an anti-climax for the Rovers, who were well-beaten by a much better side. It proved to be the last match of a successful season. With an average gate of 9,104, a substantial profit was made.

The 1945/46 season was a transitional season between the end of the war and the time that it would take to demobilise all the players from the services, with a return to full normality set for 1946/47. Clubs were only allowed to play three guest players from November, placing the emphasis on clubs using their own available players. Billy Marsden and his assistant, Jackie Bestall, had gathered a good crop of young players together and continued to look around to build the squad up. The League was reorganised for this season so that, as far as the Rovers were concerned, the pre-war Division Three North was divided into sections, with the Rovers in the Eastern Section containing ten clubs. A programme of eighteen games, eight won and four drawn, gave them fourth place. The FA Cup and a supplementary competition, the Division Three North Cup, replaced the War Cup. The FA Cup for this season was played on the two-leg system. The Rover's opponents in the first round were Rotherham United, who won both games for an overall aggregate win of 3-1. The qualifying competition for the Division Three North Cup comprised home and away matches against five other clubs. The Rovers finished at the top of their section, thereby qualifying for the competition proper.

Syd Bycroft, 1945/46.

Rovers attack the Manchester United goal at Belle Vue in the first leg of the War Cup, on 21 April 1945.

Rovers players having a snowball fight during the severe winter of 1946/47.

Their first opponents were Stockport County, and the first leg at home ended level at two goals each. The second leg at Stockport, the following week (30 March), was to go down in the record books as the longest match ever played.

Kicking off at 3 o'clock, the score was 2-2 after 90 minutes. The rules of the competition stated that in the event of a draw after ninety minutes, extra time would be played. If the scores were still level at the end of normal extra time, play would continue until one side scored a goal. This is exactly what happened. There were some amazing scenes in the play that followed the normal extra time. The teams did not change ends; there was no interval, and at the end, when approaching darkness and the smoky haze from the railway made further play impossible, players were collapsing from exhaustion. Even the referee collapsed at one stage, but after treatment was able to resume. When the game finally ended after 203 minutes because it was dark, it was all the players could do to hobble off the field. The replay took place the following Wednesday at Belle Vue; it was won by the Rovers by four clear goals. The following Saturday they met Rotherham United in the second round in a goalless first leg, eventually going out on aggregate 2-0.

At the end of February, manager Billy Marsden resigned, because he wanted to stay part-time so he could keep up his business interests. The directors were determined to get together a first-class team, and felt that the manager's job would have to be full-time. Jackie Bestall was appointed as his successor. A profit of £435 on the season gave the club a firm base to pursue their ambition of higher-grade football.

The 1946/47 season was an unqualified success. The Rovers broke many records on their way to the championship of Division Three North, with a record number of points for any division of the Football League. The following season in Division Two was disastrous as the club were relegated back to the Third Division North but not for long. In 1949/50, with Peter Doherty at the helm as player-manager, they again won promotion as champions of Division Three North. This time they settled in Division Two for eight seasons. However, Doherty resigned as manager in January 1958 and the club were relegated to the newly created Division Three at the end of that season, and went straight through to Division Four a season later in a tale of unmitigated disaster. Worse was to follow in 1962, when they finished third from the bottom of Division Four and had to apply for re-election. They were re-elected, but it had been an astonishing five years of decline.

In 1966 promotion was won to the Third Division, but they came straight down again. However, they bounced back as champions of Division Four in 1969. A stay of two seasons in Division Three ended with relegation back to the bottom division. In 1974 and 1979 they were re-elected into the Fourth Division, but two years later they finished third in the Division and were promoted to Division Three. Again, a two-year stay ended in relegation, but they bounced back immediately in 1984 as runners-up in Division Four. It was 1988 when they finished bottom of the pile in the Third Division after a four-season stay, and in the following season, 1988/89, they finished next to the bottom of Division Four. In 1987 automatic promotion and relegation for one club came into being between Division Four and the Football Conference, so the Rovers were only just saved from going down to the Conference. Their struggles continued as they once again finished one off the bottom in 1992, but would be in Division Three in 1992/93 because the formation of the Premier League necessitated the renaming of the Football League Divisions.

Right: George Little,
Doncaster Rovers, 1947/48.

Below: The Rovers players
report back for pre-season
training and inspect the pitch
at Belle Vue, July 1947.

Doncaster Rovers, 1948/49. Left to right, back row: McLean (trainer), Swallow, Ferguson, Stirland, Bycroft, Corbett, and Wands. Front row: Mitcheson, Thompson, Marriott, Todd, Calverley.

Thorne supporters ready to go to Blackpool (a Division One team) for the fourth-round FA Cup tie in January 1950. Note the pirate mascot, the nickname of the Rovers at that time – but it didn't last long!

Above: Stanley Matthews (Blackpool) evades a tackle from Doncaster Rovers' Pete Doherty in the fourth round of the FA Cup at Bloomfield Road in 1930.

Right: Len Graham, Doncaster Rovers' most capped player with fourteen caps for Northern Ireland.

Ray Harrison, Bert Tindill and Len Graham prepare for a game, 1950/51.

Trainer Jack Martin and his assistant Jack Hodgson talk to Ray Harrison, Eddie McMorran and Len Graham during a training session.

Len Graham (Doncaster Rovers) and Geoff Bradford (Bristol Rovers) vie for possession of the ball in a Division Two match at Belle Vue in the 1950s.

Tommy Martin, Ken Hardwick, Walter Jones and Len Graham on a training run, early 1950s.

Peter Doherty, Rovers player-manager, talks tactics with the team using the gravel as his board.

The Rovers players help out the groundsman by using the heavy roller on the pitch, 1951/52.

Tommy Martin evading a tackle to score the Rovers' first goal, twenty-five seconds from the interval, in their game with Swansea, February 1952.

Rovers fans travelled by train to Portsmouth for the FA Cup fifth-round tie at Fratton Park, February 1952.

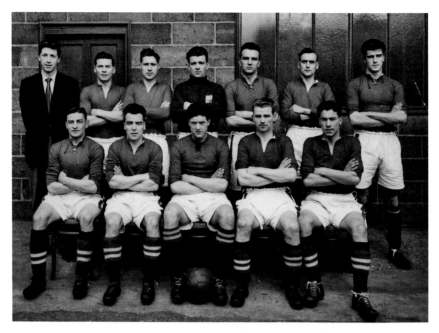

Doncaster Rovers team picture, February 1952. Left to right, back row: Herbert, W. Jones, Graham, Hardwick, Miller, Rouse, Paterson. Front row: Calverley, Kit Lawlor, Adey, Doherty, Tindill.

Doncaster Rovers team picture, March 1953 *v.* Southampton. Left to right, back row: Makepeace, T. Brown, Hardwick, Paterson, L. Graham, Teasdale. Front Row: Doherty, Adey, Harrison, McMorran, Tindill, and mascot Tony Hyde.

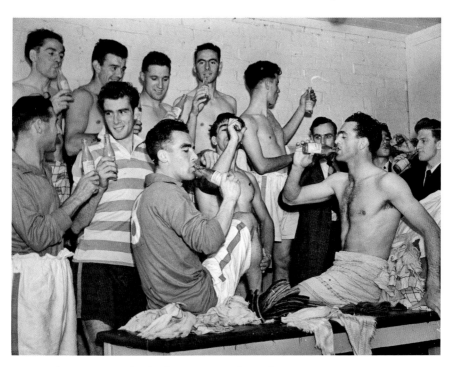

Rovers players enjoy a drink after a game in the mid-1950s.

The Rovers team, suitably attired, ready to go on their travels, 1953/54. Left to right: Bobby Herbert, Ronnie Walker, Bill Paterson, Kit Lawlor, Brian Makepeace, Johnny Mooney, Ken Hardwick, Bert Tindill, Eddie McMorran, Len Graham, Ray Harrison.

Left: Bert Tindill, 1954.

Below: Hudgell (3), Daniel and Hedley (2) of First Division Sunderland try to stop Lawlor and Walker (white shirts) of Second Division Rovers, in a famous win for the Rovers at Roker Park in the third round of the FA Cup, January 1954.

Right: Bill Paterson, 1954.

Below: Alick Jeffrey receives a birthday cake to mark his sixteenth birthday, before playing in a fourth-round FA Cup tie at home to Aston Villa, January 1955.

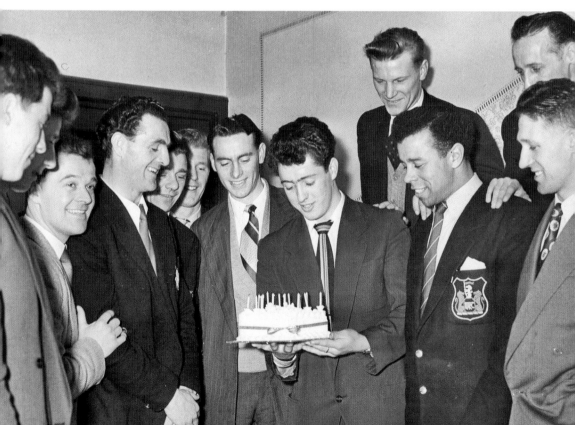

Left: Doncaster Rovers youngster Alick Jeffery heads one of the goals that knocked Aston Villa out of the FA Cup in 1955. Villa players Martin, Aldis and Baxter are left powerless.

Below: Manager Peter Doherty relaxes with his players on the grass at Belle Vue, 1955.

Right: Brian Makepeace, 1955.

Below: Doncaster Rovers, 1955/56. Left to right, back row: Brown, Rodgers, Arnold, Wallace, Graham, Gregg, Hardwick, Makepeace, Rouse, R. Walker. Middle Row: Bycroft (coach), Connolly, Palin, Gavin, Young, Williams, Herbert, Hunt, Mordue, Ewing, Hodgson (trainer). Front row: Anderson, Wood, Mooney, Tindill, J. Walker, Jeffrey, G. Walker, McMorran, Nicholson, Bryceland, and mascot Tony Hyde.

Coach Syd Bycroft takes a training session in the snow, winter 1955.

Syd Bycroft and Jack Hodgson, coaches, talk to a group of players in 1955.

Harry Gregg dives on the ball, with Len Graham standing guard and Morgan Hunt watching on, while Harold Brook (left) and John Charles (background) of Leeds United hold a watching brief at Belle Vue, April 1956.

Rovers players under the care of coaches Syd Bycroft (left) and Jack Hodgson (right).

Harry Gregg, 1956.

Charlie Williams, 1956.

A young Alick Jeffrey.

Alick Jeffrey in 1956.

Rovers 'keeper Harry Gregg fists the ball away from Leyton Orient forward Tommy Johnston, 1957.

Belle Vue in the 1970s, showing the popular stand and Rossington End.

The main stand at Belle Vue from the car park, 1970s.

Doncaster Rovers, Division Four champions, 1966. Left to right, back row: J. Watton, A. Coleman, J. Wylie, H. Fearnley, G. Ricketts, B. Kelly. Front row: T. Ogden, R. Gilfillan, L. Sheffield, J. Nicholson, A. Wilson.

Doncaster Rovers, Division Four champions, 1969. Left to right, back row: Watson, Baseldon, Flowers, Stainwright, Usher, Bird. Middle row: Mitchell, Rabjohn, Johnson, Ogston, Gavan, Wilcockson, Gray, Clish, Gilfillan. Front row: B. Barker (physiotherapist), Briggs, Regan, L. McMenemy (manager), Robertson, Webber, F. Marshall (trainer).

The new Rovers manager, Billy Bremner, and coach Cyril Knowles view the match anxiously from the old brick dugout at Belle Vue, December 1978.

An aerial view of Belle Vue in March 1979.

The 1987/88 team meet the sponsors. Left to right, back row (players only): Gaynor, Brevett, Burke, Cusack (player-manager), Deane, Rhodes, G. Humphries, R. Robinson. Front row: Stead (player-coach), C. Russell, Holmes, Joyce, Kinsella, S. Beaglehole (youth coach).

Billy Bremner (manager) and Dave Bentley (assistant manager) toast Jackie Bestall on his retirement after many years of service to Doncaster Rovers as manager and scout.

Above: Left to right: Glynn Snodin, Ian Snodin, Bill Green, Ernie Moss, John Breckin, Andy Kowalski, August 1983.

Right: Alan Brown signed for Rovers in March 1983. His son Chris signed for the Rovers nearly thirty years later, and is currently playing for the club in 2013.

Team celebrations after clinching promotion from Division Four, 7 May 1984.

Mike Collett, Peter Wetzel and John Ryan, directors 1989/90.

The Rovers in white on the attack, with Muir on the left moving inside to meet the ball, 1990/91.

Billy Whitehurst in the thick of things as he tries to win the ball, 1991/92.

In 1993, ownership of the club went into the hands of the Dinard Trading Company, with Mr Ken Richardson, a businessman from North Yorkshire, listed as the representative of the company and glorying in the title of 'consultant'. Although he hired managers to run the footballing side of things, they were really only coaches, because he actually picked the team. As things worsened, the club eventually fell through the relegation trapdoor into the Football Conference in 1998.

New owners in the guise of Westferry Ltd took over the club. They later sold it to John Ryan and Peter Wetzel, but the lease of the ground remained in their hands. The club had reached the lowest point in their recent history, as they struggled to pull away from the relegation zone of the Conference. This was achieved and the club made steady progress, finishing in a higher position each season than the one before and winning the Conference Trophy in their first two seasons. Eventually, in their fifth season in the Conference, the long-suffering fans were able to cheer them on to finish in second place in 2002/03. This season there would be a play-off to decide the second club to be promoted behind the winners of the Conference and the Rovers had won the right to be in that play-off. They beat Chester City on aggregate for the right to play Dagenham & Redbridge in a final played at the Britannia Ground, Stoke. This game went to extra time and a new innovation came into force called the 'golden goal'. The team who scored first in extra time would be declared the winner. Doncaster Rovers were that team. Dave Penney was named 'Manager of the Year' for Division Three.

Back in the Football League Division Three in 2003/04, the Rovers went from one success to another by winning the Division and promotion to Division Two or, as another renaming exercise by the Football League decreed it to be, League One, the third tier of English football. After hovering around the play-off places for most of the season, they finished in tenth place. In 2005/06, the club actually made an impact in a cup competition, the League Cup, when they reached the very fringe of the semi-final. Having beaten two Premier League teams – Manchester City and Aston Villa – on the way, in the quarter-final they came up against the mighty Arsenal at Belle Vue. With only seconds remaining in extra time, Arsenal equalised at 2-2 and went on to win the penalty shootout. In the League the Rovers finished in eighth position, just two points outside the play-off places.

The Rovers were now a force in the lower divisions, and expectations were high for further success in the following season, 2006/07. But the fans were stunned on 30 August when it was announced that Dave Penney had left the club by 'mutual consent'. Nine days later, Sean O'Driscoll, manager of Bournemouth, was appointed as successor to Penney. The fans didn't take to him straightaway, but by January, having won 'Manager of the Month' for League One, and with the Rovers in the final of the League Trophy (Johnstone's Paint), they were gradually warming to him as they realised that his way could also bring success. In fact, success came on 1 April at the Millenium Stadium, Cardiff, when Doncaster Rovers beat Bristol Rovers 3-2 in the final, with an extra-time goal from the captain, Graeme Lee.

Saturday 23 December 2006 saw the last game to be played at Belle Vue watched by 8,923 spectators as the Rovers beat Nottingham Forest by a goal from Theo Streete. The doors were then locked, and the club moved into the new Keepmoat Stadium for the New Year's Day match against Huddersfield Town, played before 14,470 fans. Mark McCammon scored the first goal and the Rovers won by three clear goals. The Rovers finished eleventh in the table that season.

Doncaster Rovers, 1994/95. Left to right, back row: Warren, Jones, Kitchen, Wilcox, Beasley, Suckling, Marquis, Roche, Brabin, Kirby. Middle row: Sibson, Limber, Thew, Maxfield, Hoy, Parrish, Harper, Lawrence, Hackett. Front row: Torfason, Gallen, Meara, Golze (youth coach), Smith (assistant manager), Chung (manager), S. Beaglehole (director of youth coaching), Finlay, P. Williams, Swailes.

Ken Richardson (benefactor) and Kerry Dixon (newly appointed manager) before the opening game of 1996/97 against Carlisle United. Ninety minutes before the match, Sammy Chung, manager, arrived at the ground, only to be told he was dismissed and Dixon appointed in his place.

RIP Rovers, 1998. Shrine left by fans in 1998 after the club was relegated to the Conference and seemingly headed for oblivion.

Joan Oldale at work in her office at Belle Vue as secretary of Doncaster Rovers.

Colin Sutherland and Ian Duerden, scorers of the goals in the second leg against Farnborough Town that won the Endsleigh Conference Trophy on 3 May 1999, celebrating with the trophy.

Dave Penney, captain, and Ian Snodin, manager, show off the Conference Trophy after the second leg of the final at Belle Vue against Farnborough Town. The Rovers had won the first leg at Farnborough with a goal from Dave Penney.

Success for the club after years of strife: the team celebrate winning the Endsleigh Conference Trophy after the second leg at Belle Vue on 3 May 1999.

The state of Belle Vue at the Town End, 2002.

Relics of the past at the Town End, 2002.

Cleaning up the derelict Town End to lay some terracing in preparation for the Football League, 2002.

The clear up of the Town End continues in preparation for terracing, 2002.

An expectant crowd on the popular side of Belle Vue, and the Sky Sports TV cameras on the 'state-of-the-art' gantry for the televised match against Dagenham & Redbridge in the Conference on 7 September 2002. This was the first-ever Rovers match to be televised live.

Keeper Matt Baker of Hereford United surrenders as he, his colleagues and Paul Barnes of Rovers wait for a corner to be taken in the match at Belle Vue in November 2002.

John Ryan makes his playing debut as a substitute for the Rovers against Hereford United at Edgar Street, the oldest player to play in senior football, at four days short of his fifty-third birthday. From left to right: Windle (physiotherapist), Tim Ryan (no relation to John), Ravenhill, Blunt, Marples, Watson, Warrington, Whitman, Doolan, Blundell, John Ryan (club owner), Barnes, Beech, Foster, Walker (assistant manager), Penney (manager).

The Britannia Stadium, home of Stoke City and venue for the first-ever Conference play-off final, between the Rovers and Dagenham & Redbridge, 10 May 2003.

The Rovers squad, suitably attired, line up for the photographers prior to the Conference play-off final at the Britannia Stadium, Stoke, in May 2003. Left to right, back row: Tierney, T. Ryan, Gill, Morley, Nelson, Warrington, Foster, Ravenhill, Green, Richardson, Albrighton, Doolan. Front row: Walker (assistant manager), Penney (manager), Marples, Watson, Windle (physiotherapist), Blundell, Blunt, Whitman.

Rovers players celebrate at the end of the Conference play-off final with exuberant fans, while a disconsolate Dagenham & Redbridge player walks away, May 2003.

Celebrations on the Britannia Stadium pitch after the Rovers had won the Conference play-off final and gained promotion to the Football League.

Dave Penney gets the signature of Michael McIndoe from the club that came up to the Football League with Rovers, Yeovil Town, August 2003.

The players inspect the pitch at Brisbane Road before the match against Leyton Orient, their first match back in the Football League, 9 August 2003.

Steve Foster, captain of Doncaster Rovers, and Matt Lockwood, captain of Leyton Orient, with the four officials and mascots from both teams, pose for the pre-match photograph, August 2003.

Doolan congratulates Green for the assist in the first goal scored by Blundell at Leyton Orient, August 2003.

Blundell on the ball to score the first goal for Rovers in their return to the Football League, against Leyton Orient, August 2003.

Chairman John Ryan presents Syd Bycoft with a memento for his services to Doncaster Rovers.

John Ryan, chairman, and Stuart Highfield, managing director, bang the drum for promotion at the home match against Darlington in March 2004.

Young Oxford United goalkeeper Simon Cox blocks a shot from Chris Brown, with Fortune-West hovering for a loose ball, at the Kassam Stadium in March 2004.

Dave Morley and John McGrath celebrate and show off the Division Three champions' silverware in May 2004.

Adebayo Akinfenwa lifts the cup as the players celebrate the winning of the Third Division as champions, and promotion to Division Two, their second promotion in two seasons.

The Rovers bench poised to run on to the pitch to celebrate being the champions of Division Three, after the last match of the season against Carlisle United in May 2004.

After the presentation of the Division Three cup and medals, Chris Brown, Dave Morley, J. J. Melligan, Tim Ryan and Adebayo Akinfenwa celebrate.

The bubbly flows in the dressing room to celebrate promotion from Division Three, and McGrath, Price and Brown show off the trophy, May 2004.

The flags are waved as the fans celebrate promotion as champions of Division Three.

James Coppinger joins Rovers from Exeter City, May 2004.

Michael McIndoe in action for Rovers against Sheffield Wednesday at Belle Vue, December 2004.

The hospitality boxes at the Town End at Belle Vue, photographed from the Rossington End.

The site of the new stadium, about half a mile away from Belle Vue, next to the Yorkshire Outlet.

Richard Offiong, Paul Heffernan – signing a programme for a young fan – and Steve Foster, 2005/06.

Michael McIndoe celebrates the scoring of the first goal – from a penalty – against Aston Villa in a Carling League Cup fourth-round tie at Belle Vue, while his teammates James Coppinger, Ricky Ravenhill and Paul Heffernan try to catch up with him, November 2005.

Somewhere in the middle of the huddle is Paul Heffernan, scorer of the second goal against Aston Villa in the Carling League Cup fourth-round tie at Belle Vue.

Paul Heffernan on the ball in the Carling League Cup fifth-round tie, while two Arsenal defenders move across to stop him, December 2005.

Neil Roberts set to take a penalty as the Carling League Cup fifth-round tie against Arsenal goes to a penalty shoot-out, December 2005.

The following season, 2007/08, O'Driscoll built the team to his own specifications, and despite a large number of injuries the team were second in the table, in an automatic promotion place after the penultimate match of the season. A win at Cheltenham Town would confirm promotion to the Championship. However, Cheltenham needed a win to save themselves from relegation, and it was they who collected the three points, with a late goal to win 2-1. The Rovers dropped to third place and the lottery of the play-offs. A comprehensive win on aggregate over Southend United put them into the final against Leeds United at Wembley on Sunday 25 May. The Rovers should have sewn the game up in the first half, but the score remained goalless at half-time. However, two minutes after the break, a corner from Stock was met with a bullet header by James Hayter into the net, and forty-three minutes later the Rovers were promoted to the Championship.

Their first season back in the second tier for fifty years started well with a win, but a run of ten defeats in twelve games left them in bottom place by November. Then the tide turned, and the second half of the season took them to fourteenth in the table and safety. The second season, 2009/10, they were favourites for relegation, but were always around the fringes of the play-off places, before faltering as the season came to an end with a final place of twelfth. A horrific series of injuries did the club no favours in 2010/11, and while they were complimented on their style of play, they could only finish fourth from the bottom by a clear six points. Dean Saunders replaced Sean O'Driscoll in September 2011, but he couldn't stem the tide, and so the club implemented a new policy. With the aid of football agent Willie McKay, former Premier League players were brought in to put themselves in the shop window. The experiment was a total failure and the club were relegated back to League One for 2012/13.

For Dean Saunders, the manager, it was back to the drawing board, with a chance to build his own team. With a much reduced budget there was a near-complete clearout of players. Consequently, the manager had to bring in players the club could afford, and it was with some trepidation that the fans awaited the start of the season. However, a good win at Walsall and a win over Bury at home augured well, but successive defeats at home to Crawley Town and away at Yeovil Town stopped any euphoria from building up. But then, in mid-September, Rovers went on an unbeaten run away from home for a joint club record of twelve games, starting with a win at Colchester, and ending, inexplicably, with a defeat against bottom club Bury at the beginning of February. They had climbed up the table to second place by early January, but had lost four League games at home during this period, which had kept them behind Tranmere Rovers.

Having reached second place on 5 January, Dean Saunders was tempted away by Wolverhampton Wanderers two days later. Brian Flynn, brought to the club as chief scout by Saunders in September, was asked to take the reins, with the captain of the team, Rob Jones, assisting with the coaching side. Life carried on and the club moved into the top spot with a win at Shrewsbury at the end of April. They held this position until the penultimate match against Notts County at home, when they lost by a single goal and were superseded at the top by Bournemouth. This left an interesting last day of the season. If Bournemouth won at Tranmere they would be champions, and if the Rovers drew against third-placed Brentford they would be promoted automatically. However, if Brentford beat the Rovers they would go up and the Rovers would be in the play-off places.

So 27 April dawned with a winner-takes-all situation at Griffin Park. Ninety minutes went by and there had been no goals, so the Rovers would be promoted with this one point. Five minutes of added time, said the referee, to some disbelief. The 94th minute came up and suddenly, in a melee in the Rovers penalty area, the referee blew and was seen to be pointing to the penalty spot. The home support was in raptures of delight; this was their ticket to promotion. Marcello Trotta took the kick, but rattled the crossbar. Desperately defending Brentford's follow-up, Furman cleared the ball to Paynter on the right touchline just inside his own half. He collected it and ran on unopposed to the edge of the Brentford penalty area. As the 'keeper came out, he squared it to the onrushing Coppinger, who had run the length of the pitch, to slot into the open net for a win. Because Bournemouth had drawn at Tranmere, Rovers would be promoted as champions of League One. Nobody inside the ground that day will ever forget an unbelievable experience, which deflated the majority but left the minority of the crowd in total euphoria.

A view from the hill of Rovers' new home at Keepmoat Stadium.

Paul Heffernan celebrates scoring his first penalty with only three minutes to go in the League game at Vale Park. He scored from a second penalty in the ninetieth minute to win the game.

Mickey Walker, caretaker manager of Rovers, with some nifty footwork at Vale Park in September 2006, in his first match in charge.

A sea of red-and-white stripes formed by the shirts worn by the fans in the West Stand at the opening game at the new Keepmoat Stadium against Huddersfield Town, New Year's Day 2007.

A panoramic view during the opening game against Huddersfield Town at the Keepmoat Stadium, the fans in the West Stand forming the red-and-white horizontal colours of the Rovers, New Year's Day 2007.

Mark McCammon just after scoring the first goal at the Keepmoat Stadium against Huddersfield Town in a League One game on New Year's Day.

The team coach, driven by John Dodsworth, drives through Cardiff on the way to the Millennium Stadium on 1 April 2007, where Doncaster Rovers faced Bristol Rovers in the Johnstone's Paint Trophy.

The toss of the coin ceremony, with Graeme Lee, captain of Doncaster Rovers, and Stuart Campbell, captain of Bristol Rovers, with the four officials, before the final of the Johnstone's Paint Trophy at the Millennium Stadium on 1 April 2007.

Manager Sean O'Driscoll leads his team out at the Millenium Stadium for the Johnstone's Paint Trophy final.

James O'Connor and Sean McDaid show off the Johnstone's Paint Trophy at the Millennium Stadium, 1 April 2007.

Paul Heffernan rifles in the second goal in the fifth minute of the Johnstone's Paint Trophy final against Bristol Rovers at the Millennium Stadium, 1 April 2007.

The Rovers players celebrate a goal in front of their own supporters, and Adam Lockwood shows what it means, in the final of the Johnstone's Paint Trophy at the Millennium Stadium on 1 April 2007.

The Doncaster Rovers train, complete with nameplate, ready to transport the fans from Doncaster to Cardiff and back again.

The Rovers' captain, Brian Stock, prepares to toss a coin in the presence of Jonathan Douglas, the Leeds United captain, the four officials and the two mascots before the League One play-off final at Wembley, 23 May 2008.

Brian Stock on the ball for the Rovers as he lines it up for a shot at goal, while Sam Hird directs operations in the rear at Wembley, 23 May 2008.

James Coppinger receives an ardent kiss from Mrs Ryan, John Ryan congratulates James O'Connor, and Lewis Guy receives his medal at the play-off final at Wembley on 23 May 2008.

Above: Brian Stock and Adam Lockwood show the League One play-off cup to the fans, while Paul Green, Gareth Roberts, Richie Wellens, James Coppinger and James O'Connor also celebrate and acknowledge the fans at Wembley, 23 May 2008.

Below: The first game in the second tier in fifty years for the Rovers, and Lewis Guy scores the first goal to win the game at Pride Park, August 2008, with James Hayter looking on approvingly.

Above: Dean Saunders meets the squad at Cantley Park for the first time after taking over from Sean O'Driscoll as manager.

Below: James Coppinger celebrates his goal at the Valley against Charlton Athletic to set the Rovers on the winning trail as the rain lashed down, March 2009.

Flares go off and players celebrate the goal that won the club the League One championship at Brentford.

Captain Rob Jones stands in the crowd at full time at Brentford.

The winning goalscorer, James Coppinger, salutes the fans at Brentford.

Tommy Spurr, Paul Keegan and John Lundstram celebrate the win.

Rovers players celebrate
with the champions'
banner at Brentford.

Above: Players celebrate winning the League One championship in the Brentford away dressing room.

Below: Iain Hume, James Coppinger, Tommy Spurr and David Syers with the champions' trophy.

Above: The Rovers' captain, Rob Jones, lifts the League One champions' trophy at Keepmoat Stadium on the Monday following the win at Brentford.

Below: Players celebrate at Keepmoat Stadium.

The winning goalscorer, James Coppinger, and manager Brian Flynn celebrate.